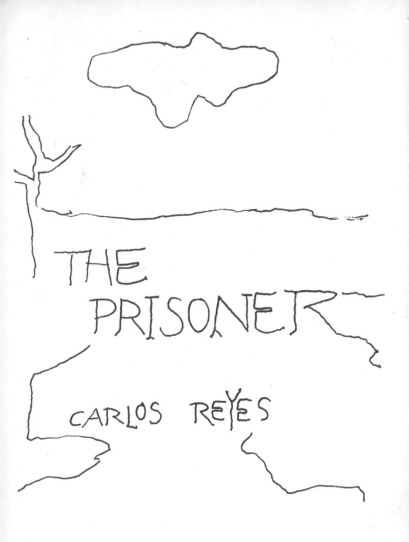

THE PRISONER

CARLOS REYES

CAPRA PRESS   1973   SANTA BARBARA

*The title pages were designed especially
for the author by Robert Duncan.*

Photograph of Carlos Reyes by Greg Heinze

Some of these poems appeared in
*The Review, The Minnesota Review,
Charlie, & Diana's Bi-Monthly*

ISBN 0-912264-62-4(pa.)
ISBN 0-912264-63-2 (Signed Hardbound)

CAPRA PRESS
631 State Street
Santa Barbara, Ca. 93101

for Michael, Amy, Nina & Cizzi

THE PRISONER

COVE

My childhood
was a natural meadow
at the top of the hill
where geese flew to a secret pond and in the full
august the moon woman would come
to gather certain flowers
also a white deer, I
came there seeking
water at six in the morning

IT IS

the clouds spread evenly underneath my teeth
the mornings I go searching underneath my comb
the twenty fifth birdless winter on brushes
hair outside in the rain the twenty five silent maidens
waiting on the day with a leaky roof I can't remember
something about crumpled bed sheets all over
    my morning
the mornings I can never seem to find
when sand covers all the clouds that ever were or werent
my teeth are in the bathroom searching for a brush
everything in need of patching up
especially the maiden repair shop where I work
on sanded off saturdays

ORCHARD

(I saw a spotted fawn

          in the wet high grass
          the day we went looking and found
          the old clydesdale caught
          in the fence.   one leg between
          barbed wires cut to the bone
          making a mud hole where his hoof

trying to escape)

THE PRISONER (2)

he feels boxed in the man
the man after him has an automatic
stapler run by
compressed air
ready to put on the third side
another man stands, impatient
to begin spray painting
the mail truck idles
out side some one will find enough money
the postage to mail him
only he knows the address
of his destination and he ain't
about to tell, nobody

THE MAIDEN REPAIR SHOP HAS A LEAKY ROOF

It is the sandy air that frightens me the clouds
when there are no clouds the mornings when I get up
to find particles small gray and flat spread over
worlds and I go searching, picking up each
   particle, hoping
to find some trace of you
underneath the bed sheets are crumpled
it is the twenty fifth of winter birds whose names I
   don't remember
silent outside.   on the bushes.   in the rain

A SPANISH POEM

It was one of those days
A day of silent trees
A day when trees were sleeping

VISIT TO A CEMETERY IN WINTER

—for harold and maude

Which exit do we now take?   The days
The sudden realization that something beautiful is
    about to happen
Too much chrome on the grill of the 1949 Mercury
The upholstery smelling of stale smoke, beer
    and fucking
A windshield wiper that won't work
The transmission that hides out incognito under
    the body
Failing.   Not failure as such, so much
Mechanical with its left shoe left on
And no sock, dead battery and dead leaves
Sunflowers springing up through cloudy windows
Like the story you couldn't tell
Whose punch line was lost among the ferns
And corrected with tiny copper bells and lost
Needles of insanity home for the week-end
Lost in the haystack of a brass bed
Where lions jump

Through polished hoops spinning a web
Behind mirrors of truth the horizon
Is always so far away
Renegade stars pretending to be boats
And passing upside down question marks
A cross is placed in every passing window
And footsteps clad in ski-boots
Dance a minuet on New Year's Day
To the tune of jig-saw puzzles and chess boards
In the junkyard ink runs out
Overheated radiators spouting like whales
Along with anti-freeze or some one reading
A newspaper printed in 1923
And cigarettes burn uneven holes
In shortened winter days
And you stare at the red lights on top of buildings
And wonder what happened
To all the laughing children

AN ODYSSEY ON FILE

like the phone call or was it
some dream you were dreaming
they beat you up, kicked in your
ribs, you roll about the floor
in agony, in anticipation, waiting
for the slug to strike you wondering
who it was that said that it was
the echo of that voice
that woke you, a telephone.   was it?
painful and why
does your ear hurt, why does the phone
stop ringing when you try to talk to it

you are left
an abacus
hanging
on the wall that nobody knows how to use

LOVE AT FIRST SIGHT

Her head appeared
through the plastic
leaves of a rubber tree plant

His was a face
of the underside of the counter
of the diner all stuck
with fifteen years
of tradition of wads of gum

He showed to her instead
his other side
an old fashioned primary school
child's desk top
where time and children
had carved

      She saw both sides at once

CROSSING THE BORDER

Like the comings and goings
into motels and out
into the night dark as the inside
of an eyeless needle
a moth flits around inside me
like a ghost that never was
he comes on shy like a little boy
and while they aren't looking
hits them with his silk gloves
leaving no bruises, according
to the newspaper accounts
they always awake dreaming
of a young man and of being raped
somewhere across town

IN THREE FRAMES

She was bathing the baby in the bathroom in the
   hallway was empty
She was getting him ready for his father
would be home soon she talked to him a lot incessant
   baby talk babble
His father would be home soon.   for sure.   it was almost
time the voice of father penetrating all
the walls saying I'm home!
finally he appears in the empty
hallway to get his father he is cleaned.   he is all dressed
his one eye as big as his head is sparkling
his shirt collar is buttoned up, tightly around the eye ball
a crystal ball perched
like a gypsy's
crystal ball
his father has brought him
something in a brown paper bag
in his eagerness
he spills it
eyeballs
roll all over the floor like glass marbles

HE

he prowls the street, a dog
his man on a leash
four miles long smelling every thing
as though it were important
to his identity

> (here a sniff
> there a sniff
> X marks the spot
> spot marks the X
> soul, yellow
> and you go to heaven)

some nights he thinks he is a dog
others that he is a man
he can't see the chain
around his neck like a wax ring
he washes his hands every five minutes
in mud puddles   in the summer
nervous he likes the rainy blacks
of night

(21)

ADAM AND EVE WENT DOWN TO THE RIVER TO PLAY

two ribs sticking out of the sand say
prayers to two buzzards who wait stomachs
shrinking the sun has turned piss yellow
one buzzard talks to the other, the other
buzzard talks to him what they say is self
not recognized, not . . a car is coming across
the desert looking for an idea
in one of those ribs like an old steam loco-
motive chugging churning up the sand dunes
all this , afantasy of 1848, 1946, 1950
old men cry when they see

ONE OF THE THINGS THAT YOU DO
AND ARE RESPONSIBLE FOR

His friendship had been
a flag waving in his youth

somewhere along tree lined streets was the carving
of your initials and his on the oldest hickory tree

he could find it, easily
like a garbanzo bean

cooked for days, care
fully but tender enough

love, for eating

. . . CLOUDS IN YOUR COFFEE

—for carly simon

The renegade horizon
lights an occasional passing
red lines burning small

boats, a memory of fireball whales
misty afternoons and sun
waiting for warm mourning

while his life disappears
like the coke in his pocket
and slushy upside down

seagulls, shooting stars and
frozen upside down questions
his eye like thirty five knots
tied together by the northeast wind

THE BIN

I stand here before you
graceless, looking guilty, feeling
like the doctor who has just attempted
to drive a balsa stake through
the heart of a vampire and as innocent
as the fourteen year old boy who has been
raped in the hallway
by a nympho who steals cigarettes
sprinkling salt in all of the flower pots
when no one is looking as
ashamed as the old woman who sits
dress up over her head talking to herself
insisting the parade is about to begin
(as soon as they burn the christmas trees
tonight *is* the night isn't it?

I stand before you running your fingers
through my hair waiting for you
to tell me what you always tell me

(25)

MARY

The moon was full
a woman
where light reflected off
a rounded hillock
a corona, a halo
around where the head of where
the future should be
a religious painting
a virgin mary or mary pregnant
jane he couldn't decide
if it was sacrilege or beautiful
her life was like that
similes and metaphors
where in context nothing fit

ROCKS

—for Richard Johnson

the rocks
dreamed of the accidental
discovery of some thing uncovered
recently under cover as it were
that undercover agent who had
under the covers reading his secret
waited breathless for the light
to self destruct under the cover of darkness
he slipped quietly away
covering up his tracks
leaving
the rocks out there confused
puzzled wondering
why he had left them
uncovered

WHY LAUGHTER IS NOT ALWAYS
THE BEST MEDICINE

> "Tengo mucho miedo
> de las hojas muertas"
> G. Lorca *Aire de Nocturno*

October must be the death of all things
That I do not fear dying, but October.
It is not October that I fear, it is
what comes after: it is winter I fear.
Winter is truly the death of all things

Today, the 26th of October, daylight saving
time ended and somewhere in the hour we lost
when we set the clock back was
the death of all things

MOON WALK / MOON TALK

—for jane hamilton

Walking up the edge of the moon
below all that glitters is not gold
clear night air on the rocky road

I throw Pablo Neruda's ode off
the mountain one rock at a time

the moon warms
the landscape and we listen carefully for coyotes
and become coyotes
yelling with our voice
de Grazia couldn't paint this

I throw another Neruda down the hill
while we talk like massive cardiacs

And Jane, there is no planet
here on this moon for hearts through beating

Why a pubis is not a Rose

> not.   a flight of birds
> feathery & full
> of beating wings.   not

II.

> ago.

She stands naked
a rose in her teeth

they are teeth & you
are all smiles you feel
good in all the right places

It is 6 a.m., 10 a.m., 11:30 a.m.

& some one is leaving
this scene.   a dream
disappearing
behind plastic curtains
never raised

where light is
& you are sleepy

& some one is leaving,
always

III.   Poem of fluttering: birds wings

There is no way to write about this
poem of fluttering.   wings.   birds
unable to fly.   something sticks
the small foot to the earth

what you think is a trapped bird
is a twitching vein in your closed fist

over you
a cloud, a cloud of black

birds at 500 feet.   your hand
cannot reach

THE WHITE KNIGHT

The white knight with cold light in his eye
as he rides forward into
winter over the countryside
the whitewash is fading
the snow that hasn't fallen is

already melting: the white knight
&   always right,
right   &   out of his mind
writing for white owls
&   the east wind

This chapbook series, edited by Robert Durand
(Yes! Press) and Noel Young (Capra Press), is de-
signed and printed by Capra Press in Santa Barbara.
This is the eighth title in the series, published
April 1973. One hundred numbered copies signed
by the author, were handbound.